Table of Contents

Introduction

When most people think of Italian recipes, pasta comes into their mind. Pasta has traditionally been an Italian recipe but it has become a popular recipe all over the world. It is a common site to see many Americans enjoying pasta recipes in an Italian restaurant.

While many people love pasta, only a few of them know how to prepare them. Many people think it is complicated to make them while it is very easy.

It is essential for having the right pasta machine when you want to prepare homemade pasta.

Pasta combines well with meat stews, vegetables and vegetable salads, and with almost any soup or sauce, without diminishing the taste, or appeal of the pasta accompaniment, but instead enhancing it.

Pasta can also easily be served to enhance the appeal of the meal and will blend in well with almost any type of garnish.

Importantly are the minimal ingredients required to prepare the dough and the commonality of the ingredients.

With some practice, fresh pasta making, should thus be a shared endeavor in your meal planning and pasta should become an ever so often meal you could prepare, for special occasions, to entertain guests and the family or simply just treat yourself to a delicious meal.

Nutritionally, pasta is mainly carbohydrates, i.e., starch, with some protein and manganese. However, kinds of pasta may contain some additions such as spinach, herbs spices, cheeses, mushrooms and various other seasonings. The net effect of these additions being to enhance the nutrition composition of the pasta, improving the nutrient contents by incorporating, vitamins, iron and other minerals found in the added ingredients.

Pasta is one of the most popular meals enjoyed by millions, no, billions of people around the world. Pasta is indeed delicious and popular around the world with almost every corner of the globe customizing a pasta recipe and enjoying it by the cultural practice of that region.

This book contains information about Italian pasta and how to prepare them. It has Italian pasta recipes categorized into short, long and stuffed pastas. There is also information on how to prepare the dough to make pasta. As you may know, the dough-making process is fundamental in making pasta.

Many of us cannot enjoy a great tasting pasta dish unless the pasta is cooked to perfection each time. If you fit into this category, don't worry—this book the perfect directions to make the ideal and tender pasta with every recipe that you make.

All recipes included in the book will only be for homemade pasta. At the same time, for cooking and sauces, Owen Conti has made another book titled Pasta Sauce Cookbook and is available on Amazon.

Chapter 1: The Various Types of Italian Pasta Dough

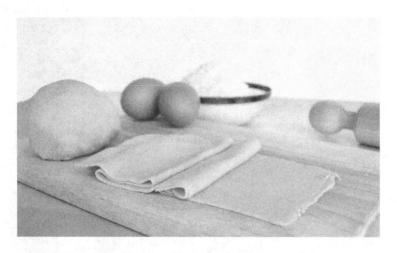

Gluten-Free Pasta Dough

Cook Time: 45 Minutes

Serves: 4

Difficulty: Difficult

Ingredients:

- 150 g gluten-free rice flour , plus more to dust

- ¼ teaspoon fine sea salt

- 1 tablespoon extra-virgin olive oil

- 1 tablespoon cornflour

- 2 tablespoons xanthan gum

- 50 g potato starch

- 3 large eggs

Preparation:

1. Process all the ingredients in a food processor to create rough dough. Dust the working surface with flour and place the dough there. Knead until the dough is smooth.

2. Divide the dough into four and then use your fingertips to press each piece. Put into a pasta machine to roll. Begin with the widest setting and then turn again.

3. Roll the pasta twice on each setting, apart from the two narrowest settings, to form a 2mm thick sheet. Place the pasta on surface dusted with flour and use a dump tea towel to cover it. Proceed for the other dough.

4. Transform the dough into pasta of your choice. Making tagliatelle, roll the pasta on that setting on the machine. You can alternatively use a knife to into strips of 7mm and put on a surface dusted with flour.

Nutritional value per serving:

Calories 273, Fats 8.1 g, Saturates 1.7 g, Sugars 0.3 g, Protein 8.9 g, Carbs 41.3 g

Fresh Egg Pasta Dough

Cook time: 30 Minutes

Serves 4

Difficulty: Medium

Ingredients:

- 600 g Tipo '00' flour
- 6 large eggs

Preparation:

1. Pour the flour on a pasta board. Make a fountain and the middle and crack in the eggs.

2. Beat the eggs using a fork until smooth. Thoroughly mix with flour.

3. Dust with flour and knead to form a silky, smooth and elastic dough.

4. Use a cling film to cover the dough and allow 30 minutes to rest in a refrigerator.

5. Roll it and shape it the way you want.

Nutritional value per serving:

Calories 620, Fats 12 g, Saturates 3 g, Sugars 2.2 g, Protein 26.7 g, Carbs 101.4 g, Fiber 3.9 g

Royal Pasta Dough

Cook time: 30 minutes

Serves: 8

Difficulty: Not too tricky

Ingredients:

- 12 large free-range eggs

- 2 tablespoons extra virgin olive oil

- 75 g fine semolina

- 400 g good quality 00 flour type, plus extra for dusting.

Preparation:

It is royal pasta dough, velvety pasta, silk, made with a pure blend of fine semolina which has a golden color and a wonderful flavor, and 00 flour (00 means super fine.) This blend of free-range egg yolks along with flours gives you the ultimate in pasta dough. The best part of it is that it's super cheap based on the pasta volume it gives you. Roll or cut into hundreds of different shapes. Enjoy and feel the joy and pride of making pasta from scratch by yourself.

The pasta world is full of old wives' tales and rules of the dos and don'ts but throughout the whole of Italy, in every town, region or village, they frequently contradict each other. This particular method gets you in the right place but you can still roll out thicker to get a thicker noodle, which you will have to cook longer. The critical question to consider is this. Will it go well with the sauce you want to pair it with? The pasta shape and the sauce should be in harmony. The pasta equals to the sauce.

The dough

Pile the semolina and flour in a bowl and scoop a well at the center. Separate the eggs and pour in the yolks. For the egg whites, put them into a sandwich bag and put them in the freezer. Keep them to make meringues the next day.

To the well, add 4 tablespoons water and the oil and using a fork, whip up with the eggs until they are smooth and bring the flour gradually.

Clean your hands and flour them and get them in there and bring the dough together to form a ball when it becomes too hard to mix. Dust a work surface with flour and knead for about 4 minutes until elastic or smooth. Flour can differ in humidity and eggs differ in size. The dough should not be too dry or too wet. Add more flour or water if you desire. Cover with a cling film and allow about 30 minutes to rest.

Rolling out

Customarily, Italians used to have a giant rolling pin. If you like you also can do it in that way but it requires some elbow grease and a large flat surface. In this modern era, it's advisable and fun using a pasta machine. For a machine, firmly fix the machine to a clean and nice table and cut the pasta dough in four pieces and so that it does not dry out as you proceed. Cover it with a damp clean tea towel.

Stage 1

Flatten every piece of the pasta dough one at a time and run in on the thickest setting and take down the rollers by two parameters and then rerun the dough to get a thinner one. You can fold it into two and run it back again on the thickest setting. If you repeat this several times, it makes the dough very smooth and turns it into one that will fill the pasta machine out from a tatty sheet.

Stage 2

Roll the pasta sheet down on every setting and flour a little as you proceed. To avoid any ripples, folds or kinks, use one hand to turn the crank while maintaining a low tension with the other side. Take it down until you obtain the thickness you desire which is supposed to be 2 mm for shapes like tagliatelle, Lasagna and linguine. For tortellini and ravioli turned into filled pasta, go for a thinness of 1 mm because it doubles to 2 mm when folded around a filling.

Chestnut Pasta Dough

Ingredients:

- 200 g Whole wheat flour

- 400 g Chestnut flour

- 6 eggs

- 1 pinch of salt

- 200 g 00 flour

Equipment:

- Pasta maker

- Rack

- Rolling pin

Farina di Castagna is the Italian chestnut flour that we use to make this delicious recipe. This flour is very well ground and the ideal pasta flour. With a pasta maker, things are going to be quite easy for you.

For this pasta, you start by mixing chestnut flour and whole wheat flour and make a well at the center. Add eggs and salt and use your hands to mix. Knead to form dough that is soft and then cover and allow 30 minutes to rest.

Use a pasta maker to roll the dough as possibly thin and cut into shape of choice.

If you will not immediately cook the pasta, dust it with flour or semolina and place it on a rack to dry.

Buckwheat Pasta Dough

Ingredients:

- 125 ml water

- 2 egg whites

- 300 g Buckwheat flour

Equipment:

- Freezer

- Tray

- Table

STEP 1 - By hand

You can make this pasta dough using buckwheat and egg yolks. You start by mixing the flour and the egg yolks. Make a well in the middle and add water. For this dough you don't add salt. Use your hands to knead the dough, adding water if it is too dry. The dough should be smooth and shouldn't stick on your fingers.

Dust a table with flour and place the dough there.

STEP 2 - With Regina

Insert some dough in the Regina hopper. Turn the crank. After some time, the pasta comes out. When it gets to the length you want, use a slicer to cut.

Repeat the process for the remaining dough. Dust a tray or a cloth with flour and place the pasta there.

You can store the pasta in a freezer, and eat within a month.

Homemade Red Pasta Dough

Ingredients:

- 3 Large eggs

- 1 pinch of salt

- 2 ½ cups type 00 flour

- 1 tbsp. water

- ½ tbsp. tomato pastel

- 3 egg yolks

Equipment:

- Tray

- Bowl

- Plastic wrap

- Pasta machine/rolling pin

- Refrigerator

This pasta is made red by adding some tomato paste. You start by the flour to a tray or working surface and make a well in the middle. You then crack in the eggs, add tomato paste and salt and mix. Add in water little by little and knead using hands until dough is smooth and soft.

Form a ball and put it in bowl and use a plastic wrap to cover. To make it firm, put in a refrigerator for 30-60 minutes.

The next thing is to use the pasta machine to roll the dough into shape of choice. Alternatively, you can use a rolling pin.

Homemade Whole Wheat Pasta Dough

Ingredients:

- 200 g 00 flour

- 2 ¼ cups, white whole wheat flour

- 1 yolk

- 4 eggs

- ½ tsp. sea salt

Equipment:

- Rolling pin

- Pizza cutter/Knife

- Damp towel

- Electric crank

This recipe requires just three ingredients; white whole-wheat flour, eggs and salt. Just like with many pasta recipes, you start mixing the ingredients on a flat surface and making a well at the center. Crack in the eggs and add salt and mix. Knead with hands to form smooth and soft dough. When done, use a damp towel to cover and allow 30 minutes to rest.

Cut the dough into 8 pieces and use hands to flatten each of them and of course dusting each with flour. Roll the dough into thin sheets using a hand or electric crank. Unlike many other pasta doughs, in this one you proceed to make noodles using fettuccine attachment. You can also cut into strips of a quarter inch using a pizza cutter or a knife. Repeat until the dough is finished.

Tip:

You can use a rolling pin if you do not have an attachment to flatten the pasta into thin sheets.

Flour and Water Pasta Dough

Ingredients:

- 50 ml water

- 100 g All-purpose flour

Equipment:

- Fork

- Pasta machine

- Wooden gnocchi board

It is the most straightforward pasta dough to make. You simply mix the water and the flour and form dough. You add more water if it is too dry and little flour if it is too sticky.

On a flour-dusted surface, knead together and divide it into pieces. Mold them into the shapes you desire. For gnocchi, use hands and roll the piece's sausage-like parts of thickness of about 1.5 cm. Roll them on a wooden gnocchi board that ridges and if you do not have one, you can roll on a back of a fork.

Alternatively, you could use a pasta machine to roll them and make fettuccine or tagliolini. You can as well form strozzapreti by rolling small pieces on your palm.

Green Pasta Dough

Ingredients:

- 40 g Boiled, steamed and drained spinach

- 400 g All-purpose flour or 00 flour and more for rolling out

- 3 large eggs

- 2 pinches of salt

Equipment:

- Pasta machine/ Rolling pin

- Refrigerator

- Plastic wrap

- Stand mixer

The difference between this pasta and the others is that it is green in color. The green color is got from spinach. You start by blending cooked spinach and eggs for 10 minutes. Mix the salt, flour and spinach/egg mixture in a stand mixer until a ball is formed. Add flour is the dough is sticky or water a tablespoon at a time if it is dry. Do this until you get smooth and homogenous dough. Use a plastic wrap to cover it and refrigerate for half an hour.

Divide into four pieces and flatten them into rectangles and flour every part on every side. Put one piece into the pasta machine. Fold the ends inside and put it into the machine once again. Proceed with the remaining dough. By the way, you can use a rolling pin if you do not have a stand mixer but make sure that you flour the working surface well.

Dust a work surface with flour and place the pasta sheets there for about 10 minutes to dry. Fix the fettuccine accessory and put one layer through the machine. Proceed with the remaining pasta. Ensure that the fettuccine ribbons floured well, so avoid them sticking together. You can alternatively use hand in fettuccine to cut the pasta sheet.

Basic Orecchiette Pasta Dough

Ingredients:

- 11/2 cups, All-purpose flour, unbleached

- 1 cup semolina flour

- 2/3 cup, warm water

Equipment:

- Plastic wrap

- Rolling pin/Pasta machine

- Knife

- Dish towel

- Disk

- Jars

- Baking sheets

You can make this dough with sauce of uncooked basil and tomatoes, broccoli rabab sauce or ice cream sauce with mint and mussels. You start by mixing flours and making a well in the middle. Add water a teaspoon at a time as you stir with your hand. Continue until you get smooth and soft dough.

Dust a working surface with flour and kneed you get a supple and smooth result. Cut a piece of the dough the size of a golf ball and then use plastic wrap to cover the remaining dough. Roll to form a cylinder using a pasta machine or a rolling pin into a diameter of one inch. Slice the cylinder using a knife into 3mm thick disks.

Get a disk and press it on the palm of your hand and use the thumb of the other hand to press. Swivel your hand two times to make the center of the ear thinner and let the rim to be a bit thicker. Place it on a clean dishtowel. Repeat for the remaining dough. Once done, drizzle some flour on the ears and repeat until all dough is finished.

To store the pasta, spread the rounds on baking sheet with flour. Leave them overnight at room temperature. Once dry, store the orecchiette in covered jars at room temperature.

Pici Pasta Dough

Ingredients:

- 1 ¾ cups All-purpose flour

- 1 tbsp. olive oil

- 1 cup semolina flour

- 7/8 cup, water

- A pinch of salt

Equipment:

- Fork

- Plastic wrap

- Refrigerator

- Rolling pin/ Pasta machine

- Knife

For this recipe, you start by mixing salt and the flours and then making a well at the middle. Add oil and then water, a little by little. Use a fork to start forming dough. Switch to using your hand to mix the dough and then knead until it is smooth and soft. Use a plastic wrap to cover and let it rest for an hour, or you can alternatively refrigerate for up to one day.

Form the dough into a round shape and cut into four pieces. Use a plastic wrap to cover the pieces. Dust a working surface with flour to get it ready. Use your hand to flatten a piece of dough and dust with flour. Roll using a rolling pin and slice into quarter inch lengths.

To make pici, you roll the edges inwards in order to keep them moist. If your environment is dry, make sure that you cover with a plastic wrap or a cloth. Use a knife to cut a round piece and use a rolling pin to roll the pasta outwards from the middle to a diameter of ¼ inch. Make the pici as skinnier as possible.

A pici that is finished should be 8-inches long, You can also elongate them up to 18 inches. Do not make it any longer. Lay them on semolina or cornmeal-dusted pasta and use a cloth to cover when a sheet is complete.

Bigoli Pasta Dough

Ingredients:

- 3 eggs (You can as well use duck eggs)

- 400 g 00 flour or cake flour

- 1 tsp. salt

- 2 tbsp. water

Equipment:

- Cylinder

- Fork

You start by mixing eggs and flour using a fork until clumps are formed in the flour. Use hands to mix while adding water and flour where need be. Transfer to a flour-dusted working surface and knead the dough. Ensure that press is floured in the cylinder, as bigoli is customary prepared using it. Twist it and then cut two times for a dough load off one cylinder. You will have to use your flour sparingly so that the pasta does not stick. The dough should be hard and smooth.

Corzetti Pasta Dough

Ingredients:

- 200 g semolina flour

- 200 g plain flour

- Water or dry white wine

- 4 fresh eggs

- 1 pinch of salt

- 1 tsp. extra virgin olive oil

Equipment:

- Fork

- Wooden cutting board

- Rolling pin/Pasta machine

- Cutter

- Kitchen towel

- Knife

For this dough you start by combining the semolina flour and the plain flour in a wooden bowl or wooden cutting board. Form a well at the center and add eggs, salt and the extra-virgin olive oil.

Little by little, incorporate the flours and eggs using a fork until dough starts forming. Switch to using your hands and knead the dough till it does not stick and is elastic. Add flour if the dough is too wet and add water if it is too dry. Allow about 30-40 minutes to rest.

Use a rolling pin to roll the dough to a thickness of 1 mm. Use the cutter on the corzetti stamp or a knife and cut many rounds as you are able to. Place one round on the corzetti stamp and press the stamp edges using your hand to perfectly fit the pasta in. press the pasta disk using a handle of the corzetti stamp and turn on both directions.

Place the corzetti on a parchment or kitchen towel. Set them to dry if you are not cooking immediately.

Garganelli Pasta Dough Recipe

Ingredients:

- 4 eggs

- Pinch of salt

- 1 ½ cup semolina flour

- ½ cup All-purpose flour

- Extra flour for dusting

Equipment:

- Special pin/ Simple chopstick/ Round wooden pencil

- Rolling pin/Pasta machine

- Fridge

- Plastic wrap

- Fork

- Wooden table

Mix the flours on a wooden surface and make a well at the middle and add in salt and beaten eggs. Use a fork to incorporate the mixer until it is crumbly. If you do not mind, you can use your hands too.

Use your hands to knead until the dough is elastic, smooth and soft. Cover with a plastic wrap and allow about 15-35 minutes to rest. You can alternatively store overnight in a fridge.

Cut a piece of dough and use you hand to flatten it a bit. On a flour-dusted surface, roll the dough using a rolling pin. If you have a pasta machine, pass the dough on the widest setting and fold it into half before passing it again through the pasta machine on the same setting. Change the setting to about 1 mm thickness and put each piece into the machine. Dust a working surface with flour and set the ready sheet there.

Cut every sheet into a square of 1.5x1.5 inches and allow about 15-20 minutes to dry. This prevents garganelli from being flat when ready.

To shape the garganelli, you start by placing the pasta square on gnocchi board, which is floured. Fold a square corner over the pin off the garganelli. You can alternatively use a round wooden pencil or a simple chopstick if you do not have special pin.

Roll using the pin applying pressure so as to imprint ridges and seal the garganelli. Repeat the process until the squares are finished and eventually the remaining dough.

Garlic & Parsley Pasta Dough

Ingredients:

- 2 cups 00 flour

- 1 bunch, Fresh parsley

- 1 tsp. salt

- ½ cup, water

- 2 garlic cloves

- 4 eggs

- 40 g garlic puree

- 1 tsp. olive oil

Equipment:

- Rolling pin

This pasta dough is quite easy. You start by combining egg, flour, salt, olive oil, chopped parsley and garlic. Knead the mixture until you get smooth and soft dough. Allow about 15 minutes for the dough to rest for making your pasta.

Yellow Flour Pasta Dough

Ingredients:

- 150 g Corn flour

- 5 eggs

- 1 yolk

- 250 g 00 flour

- Salt

Equipment:

- Fork

- Plastic wrap

This dough appears yellow in color. You start by pouring the flour on a clean working surface and making a well at the middle. Crack in the egg and use a fork to incorporate slowly until it starts to be clumpy. Switch to using your hands and keep kneading until you the dough form up. Scrap and discard any dried bits of dough and put them away.

Dust a working surface with some flour and knead the dough until it is smooth, soft, and not sticky. Divide it into 9 pieces that are equal and use a plastic wrap to cover them. Store the while covered at room temperature until you are ready to prepare them. You can also form into shapes of choice if you desire.

Chapter 2: How to Prepare the Dough

There are two major types of pasta dough in Italy:

Simple Pasta With Eggs

This pasta dough includes eggs and to prepare it, get a wooden board and on it pour the flour. In the middle, make a well and add eggs and get a fork for using to mix them. Once the mixture begins getting thick, you can begin using your hand and vigorously knead using the palm of your hands. Do this until you get homogeneous and smooth dough. You can now shape your dough into your desired pasta shapes.

When making egg-based pasta, eggs play a fundamental role in your success rate:

- Use only fresh eggs, of the highest possible quality.

- Break the eggs into a separate bowl before adding them to the flour to make sure they are not spoiled.

- For best results, bring the eggs to room temperature before using them in your dough.

- When making egg pasta dough, always use large eggs with an average weight of about 2 ounces each.

Flour and Water Pasta Dough

Pasta dough with flour and water is one of the simplest to make. All you need to do is to mix the flour with the water and make dough. If the dough is too sticky, you can add a little flour and if it's too dry, you can add a little water.

Go on a surface that has been flour dusted and use your hands to knead. Knead continuously until you get smooth and elastic dough. Mold them in the pasta shapes you want.

Ingredients:

- 1 tablespoon olive oil

- 1 2/3 cups Italian 00 flour

- 2 large eggs

- Pinch sea salt

Preparation:

1. Put the flour on a clean pastry board and make a well at the middle using your fist.

2. In the well, break eggs and put them, also add oil and a pinch of salt. If you want to color your dough, at this point you can add the ingredients

3. Using a fork, mix the eggs into the flour until it becomes clumpy. Switch to using your hands to form a firm dough by bringing the ingredients together. Add some few drops of water if the dough is too dry and if too wet, add a little more flour. As time goes on you get used to how dough should feel after making it for several times. Note that your

pasta will taste floury and be tough if you add to much flour.

4. Knead the pasta dough for 2 to minutes until its smooth. Massage the dough lightly with olive oil. Use a resalable plastic bag and tuck the dough and leave it to rest at room temperature for at least 30 minutes. The dough will be more elastic than it was before after resting.

Passing the pasta dough through the pasta machine

1. You can choose to use a long wooden rolling pin to roll the dough into a pasta machine is better and makes the work less.

2. Set the machine on widest setting and feed the blob of pasta dough through the machine. When the pasta dough sheet comes out, fold it starting from the edges pass it into the rollers again on that widest setting. Pass it several times on the widest setting. This replaces kneading the dough and ensures the pasta is smooth and silky.

3. Repeatedly pass the dough sheet through the machine and reducing the setting slowly until you get the thickness you desire. If you unable to keep the dough from folding on

itself since the sheet of pasta dough tends to become long, you can cut the sheet of dough in halves and separately feed through every half.

4. When you get the desired thickness, hang it of the back of a chair or over a broom handle for it to dry a little. This makes cutting easier as it's not stick especially in humid weather. However, if you are in a hurry, you can use a little flour to dust the pasta and let it rest for just a short time on clean kitchen towels.

5. You can now shape the dough in your desired pasta

Fresh Egg Pasta (Puff Pastry and Shapes)

Prep time: 15 minutes

Serves: 4

Difficulty: Easy

Cost: Very low

Ingredients:

- 4 organic eggs

- 400 g 00 flour

Preparation:

1. To prepare fresh pasta, pour flour on a wooden pasta board or a bowl (a wooden board is preferred). Make a well at the middle and add in eggs and use a fork to mix them. When it starts becoming thick switch to using hands and knead vigorously with the palm of your hand until the dough becomes smooth.

2. Use a tablecloth or a cling film to cover the dough and allow a minimum of 30 minutes at room temperature to rest.

3. Use a tarot to cut a piece of the dough and leave the rest covered. Flour the piece and use a dough sheeter to pull it

to the maximum thickness. Get the dough and pass between rollers to form thick dough.

4. Fold from the edges towards the middle and drizzle with some little flour. Pass it between rollers again until a rectangular sheet is formed. Flour a surface and lay the sheet there and use a knife or a tarot to trim the edges. Divide the sheet into two, occasionally passing the thinnest to the thickest. Your pasta is ready.

STORAGE

You store the pasta in a freezer in shape of choice in a tray for a few hours for them to harden. When hard, transfer them to frost bags and return them to the freezer. To use you start by adding them to boiling water and continue as per instructions.

TIPS FOR GREAT FRESH PASTA!

1. It is better using a pastry board because the wooden surface is rough which is better than a surface that is smooth.

2. Use a fork to beat the eggs into the well to avoid them coming out.

3. You can add a pinch of salt if you desire.

4. Do not use currents as it makes the pasta dry.

5. Egg-flour ratio should be one egg to 100 g of flour.

6. Processing: you must take a minimum of 10 minutes to process the dough, using the palm of your hand and occasionally beat on the board to improve its elasticity.

7. Always ensure that the dough that is not being worked on is covered to avoid it drying.

8. Dust the work surface to prevent the pasta from sticking to the working surface.

9. It is advisable to dry the semolina drizzled spreadsheets on every side some minutes before you fold them to roll that is flat in case you need to make quadrucci, pappardelle, tagliolini, tagliatelle or lasagna.

10. Yolks or eggs? You can unbalance them when making stuffed pasta like tortellini or ravioli. For 140g flour, add yolk+ egg. For dry pasta, use a whole egg only.

How to Prepare Fresh Homemade Pasta

Fresh homemade is not just food! It has become a way of life both in Italy and in the rest of the world. It has been passed from one generation to another in people's families; it is a moment of happiness and celebration with friends and family. The fresh pasta is an Italian tradition that has been there for decades.

 Making fresh pasta takes patience, attention and time; to get that pasta with pleasant roughness, right consistency and cooking it right.

Macaroni, orecchiette, ravioli, lasagna or tagliatelle are way much tastier when homemade. They are also easy to prepare. You just need some few ingredients that are also easily available at the stores.

The exact place of origin of pasta is not known because there have been many places that have been alleged to be the origin of pasta. There is an assumption that the pasta discovery was a slow process. From a mix of water and crushed wheat to the discovery of bread and pasta. The fresh pasta originated from the Mediterranean and Asia.

The making of fresh homemade pasta in Italy varies from South to North. In Southern and Central Italy, the dough is prepared using water and durum wheat semolina which has been re-milled; trofie,

51

bucatini, cavatelli, orecchiette, macaroni are examples. In the northern part, the homemade pasta is usually soft and made with eggs and flour. Stuffed pasta, pici, bigoli, cannelloni, garganelli and lasagna are examples.

Any dough type chosen makes a variety of shapes. as soon as you have rolled your pasta out and cut it into shape of choice, you can cook right away.

Add some extra virgin olive oil to the water when cooking to ensure that the fresh pasta does not stick as you cook. It is also advisable not to use a colander when draining, but instead use a perforated ladle. The final result can be spoiled by colander.

There are several sauces with which you can serve the pasta with. They include meat, Mediterranean dressing vegetables, fish and many more.

How to prepare the dough for fresh homemade pasta?

Traditionally, the dough that has been used to make egg pasta. The ingredients quantities vary depending on the pasta type you want to prepare. With the recipe below, you are going to know how to make egg dough that is perfect:

Ingredients:

- 4 eggs

- 400g flour 00

- Salt

Preparation:

1. Start by pouring the flour on a pastry board and form a well at the middle. Add salt and break in the egg into the well.

2. Use a fork and start incorporating the mixture starting from the edges nearby until it starts to be clumpy.

3. Switch to using your fingers and ensure that you have incorporated all the flour into the eggs.

4. When the dough starts becoming consistent, use your hands, pulling it in all directions back and forth. Lift it off the pastry board and scrape off any bits of dough stuck on the sides using a spatula and knead it.

5. After vigorously kneading for about 10 minutes, form a ball and use a plastic wrap to cover it. Let the dough rest for about 30 minutes.

6. Cut a small piece of the dough and use your hands to flatten it into a disk. Dust the work surface with flour and place the disc on top. Use a rolling pin, moving it in every direction, to make it into the thickness you desire.

   If you have a pasta machine, pass the disk on the rolls. Fold it into 2 layers and pass it through the rollers to thin it. You can repeat the process in order to get regular shape and the thickness you desire.

7. To form tagliolini and tagliatelle or other classic cuts, roll the sheet from the edges.

8. Cut the dough using a sharp knife into 3mm thick strips for the tagliolini and 1cm thick strips for the tagliatelle. You can alternatively use a machine and cut the dough into the format you want.

9. Your pasta is now ready and you cook immediately if you desire or store.

Tips

1. To make water and flour pasta, you use the same procedure as the one above; however, in the well at the middle of the flour, add lukewarm water and a pinch of salt. The water:

flour ratio should be 1:2. Using durum wheat semolina other than flour results to a cook-resistant pasta. You can get pastas like trofie, bucatini, cavatelli, corzetti, orecchiette etc. using this dough type. All these have a sustained thickness and should not be left so much al dente when you cook them.

2. To make the green pasta, you use the same preparation steps for egg and flour pasta dough. What you need to pay attention to most is the ingredients doses: decrease the water and egg quantity as vegetables have water in them; furthermore, it is advisable using very few egg yolks to ensure the green color is retained by the pasta.

Chapter 3: The Most Important Tools Used to Make the Dough

The Art of Italian Fresh Pasta

This art of making the homemade pasta is very crucial in the Italian tradition. Even though the fresh pasta recipes always vary from one region to another for example the type of flour, water, eggs, salt and olive oil, all are elements that may be there or not even there and are also in various quantities. The common thing in this practice of ancient times that was born in families that used simple ingredients and tools.

In the modern world, this tradition is practiced less in the families as many Italian women work more form outside the home. Good enough this practice is still alive in the grand mothers and is mostly applied by companies, restaurants and specialized schools.

Who is known as a puff pastry? This is a person who makes handmade pasta traditionally using a rolling pin and a wooden board. This is a traditional name. It used to be an informative and fun way. The tools below are great and aid in making perfect homemade fresh pasta.

Essential Tools

These are the tools that you really can't make pasta without. But don't panic! Most of these are items you already own.

Pasta Machine

This is a very useful piece of equipment to have, especially if you are planning to make pasta often or for more than two people. It saves you a lot of time and effort, as it does the rolling for you, and it also ensures a uniform thickness to the pasta sheets. You can get a manual machine or a motorized one. I have a manual one and I love it, but the choice is yours. Pasta machines often come with attachments to cut pasta ribbons, like tagliatelle and/or tagliolini, which are very useful too.

Baking Sheets

You need three baking sheets (10 by 15 inches in size) on which to place your ready pasta before cooking it. Make sure to always dust the baking sheets with a couple of tablespoons of flour so that the pasta doesn't stick to the surface.

Big Wooden Board

You need a big wooden board or at least a big wooden cutting board to give pasta like orecchiette and strascinati their characteristic rough surface to which the sauce clings.

Rolling Pin

Using a rolling pin to roll out pasta both non-egg and egg is very relaxing. A long, thin, European-style rolling pin is useful when making pasta that requires rolling out, like ribbon pasta, for example. It is essential if you do not have a pasta machine.

Cookie/Pasta Cutters

Cookie cutters can be very useful when making stuffed pasta. You need a heart-shaped cookie cutter to make hearts and a star-shaped cookie cutter to make stars. You also need round pasta/cookie cutters to make different shapes of stuffed pasta. You will need one each of 1½-inch, 2½-inch, 3-inch, and 5-inch diameters. Alternatively, you can use a glass or a bowl of the same diameter as a guide and a no serrated knife to cut around it.

Kitchen Scale

Making pasta from scratch is very easy when you have the right dough, and to obtain the right dough, the best thing to do is to precisely weigh the ingredients. This is particularly important when you are just starting out and are not yet familiar with the correct look and feel of good pasta. A weighing scale is a really important tool when it comes to pasta making, and I highly recommend you use one.

Knives

You need a good, sharp, no serrated cutting knife to cut out your dough and turn it into pasta or gnocchi. You'll use a round-edged table knife to give pasta like orecchiette and corzetti its typical shape.

Crinkle-Edge Pastry Wheel and/or Pizza Cutter

You need a crinkle-edge pastry wheel to make stuffed pasta, like ravioli or caramelle, look prettier, and you also need it to give ribbon pasta, like mafalde and rombi, its characteristic shape. In some cases, a pizza cutter can be used instead of a crinkle-edge pastry wheel or a knife. You can cut out more pasta in less time if you use one.

Knitting Needle

You need a knitting needle size 0 or 1 to make pasta like maccheroni al ferretto, fusilli avellinesi, or busiati.

Metal Cake Spatula

You need a round-edged metal cake spatula to give pasta like Strascinati its typical shape. It serves the same purpose as a table knife, but it is much bigger and better suited for broader shapes of pasta. You can use it instead of the specific tool to make Strascinati, which is very hard to find.

Plastic Wrap

Plastic wrap is essential to keep your dough from drying out. Make sure to always wrap the dough tightly with plastic wrap before leaving it to rest. You should also use it to cover the dough whenever you are not working on it. If the dough dries out, it will create a crust and start breaking, and it will not be possible to shape it anymore.

Potato Ricer

A potato ricer is very useful for making gnocchi. It processes the potatoes (and other vegetables) by forcing them through a sheet of small holes, giving a smoother texture to the mash, which in turn gives you much smoother and more uniform gnocchi dough.

Non-Essential Tools

The following tools are nice to have and come in handy for making specialty pasta shapes, but they are by no means necessary.

Big Bowl

You may use a bowl to bring together all your dough ingredients before transferring it onto your work surface to knead it.

Dough Scraper

A dough scraper is a tool used to manipulate dough and to clean the surfaces on which the dough has been worked. It is generally a small sheet of stainless steel (approximately 3 by 5 inches) with a handle of wood or plastic. It can be very useful when making pasta dough, but it's not essential.

Gnocchi Board

A gnocchi board is a small wooden board with ridges that give gnocchi their traditional shape. If you can find it, the one that comes with the mini rolling pin is also perfect for making garganelli. This tool is inexpensive and a great gadget to have, but it is not essential. If you don't have one, you can use a fork to give gnocchi their typical ridges.

Food Processor

If you have a food processor, you can use it to blend all the ingredients to bring the dough together until the flour looks like coarse breadcrumbs. Then you can transfer the mixture onto the work surface and knead it.

Pasta Frame and Drying Rack

A pasta frame is a wooden frame fitted with a thin mesh. It's used to keep short pasta to dry. A drying rack is used to hang long pasta to dry.

Stand Mixer

If you have a stand mixer, you can use it to make your dough. You will need both paddle and hook attachments to bring the dough together and knead it.

Dry Pasta Stand

This dryer is exclusively designed for long fresh pasta shapes. You can be able to hang your tagliolini, pappardelle, spaghetti and tagliatelle on the guitar. When you hang them there, they dry well and won't stick to each other and will be perfect when the cooking time comes.

64

Chapter 4: Long Pasta Recipes

Scialatielli

Prep time: 15 minutes

Serves: 6

Difficulty: Very Easy

Cost: Very low

Ingredients:

- 1 egg

- 175 g whole milk

- Basil

- 10 g, extra virgin olive oil

- 30 g grated pecorino

- 400 g durum wheat semolina

Preparation:

How to prepare the scialatielli

1. Wash and dry the basil leaves and chop them finely with a knife. Pour the durum wheat in the bowl and add the beaten egg with the use of a fork.

2. Add the chopped basil, the grated pecorino and flush at room temperature after adding the milk.

3. Pour in the extra virgin olive oil and start kneading using the hand.

4. After transferring the mixture onto the pastry board, continue kneading again by hand for like 8 minutes.

5. Get homogeneous and smooth dough; leave it to rest for about 30 minutes at room temperature after wrapping it in a cling film.

6. Divide the dough into two 10s, and keep the other half, wrap it in a plastic wrap so as to prevent it from drying out because of the air. On the pastry board, work on the first part flour it with semolina using a rolling pin of about 5 mm thick.

7. After sprinkling the pastry with more semolina, drag the edges towards the center by rolling them form one side to the other till you reach the center.

8. Cut the dough into rings about 1 cm thick using a well-sharpened blade. With the help of your hands, unroll them gently. They must be like 12-15 cm long.

9. At such a point, your scialatielli are ready to be cooked in plentiful boiling and salted water for like 5 minutes.

STORAGE

You can prepare the scialatielli and allow them to dry by air for few minutes. Keep them on a try with a cloth that is floured with semolina.

You may as well freeze the dough. In such a case, pull and cut the dough to get nests that you will put on a tray with the dish towel. Put them in the frost bags for food once they are frozen.

ADVICE

How can you season this institution of Campania cuisine? With seafood cooked together in a pan with some cherry tomatoes for taste enhancement. You can as well try a vegetarian and white version like with sautéed courgettes.

Tagliolini Fatti in Casa (Homemade Tagliolini)

Prep time: 30 minutes

Cook time: 5 minutes

Serves: 4

Difficulty: Easy

Cost: Very low

Ingredients:

For fresh pasta:

- 2 medium eggs

- Semolina for pastry board

- 200 g 00 flour

Preparation:

1. Pour the flour in a bowl, add eggs and mix with a fork. Use your hands to mix until you create a homogeneous mixture.

2. Take the dough to a work surface that is lightly floured and continue working vigorously.

3. If necessary, add a little flour and work until the dough is elastic and smooth.

4. Make a ball and wrap it in a plastic wrap or put it in a food bag in a dry and cool place at room temperature for like 30 minutes.

5. When the rest time is over. Take the pasta sprinkled with little flour and divide in two parts. To avoid drying, close the film you aren't using immediately. You can pull the other using the machine or rolling pin from the lowest to the highest till you acquire a very thin sheet.

6. Put the obtained strips on a work surface, lightly floured with refilled semolina, which you can as well use to sprinkle the pasta sheets. From each sheet, make 3 rectangles and let each side dry for like 3 minutes. Without pressing, wrap the rectangles on themselves to form small rolls and use a knife to cut them into 2 mm thick strips.

7. Taking a piece of pasta, unroll the tagliolini delicately. Roll into a nest and let them dry on a clothesline or a lightly and clean floured dish towel. Continue that process till you finish all the fresh pasta.

STORAGE

It is usually better to immediately consume the tagliolini or else it can be kept for a day in the refrigerator.

You can freeze the tagliolini raw. On a tray, put the well-spaced nests of pasta and put them in a freezer for some hours so that they can harden. Put them in frost bags once they harden and place them back in the freezer. Once you want to use them, directly boil them in boiling water from frozen.

Pappardelle Fatte in Casa (Homemade Pappardelle)

Prep time: 30 minutes

Cook time: 10 minutes

Serves: 3

Difficulty: Low

Cost: Low

Ingredients:

- 3 eggs

- 300 g 00 flour

Preparation:

1. To prepare the homemade pappardelle, put the flour in a bowl or on the work surface. Break the eggs and lightly beat them using a fork.

2. Add flour to the eggs until they have absorbed the flour and on a work surface or table, start kneading using the hand. Use the palms pf your hands to work until you obtain a smooth and homogenous mixture.

3. This operation takes quite some time. To prove that all is in the right place, cut it into halves and when you see air bubbles, just know you have done a great job.

4. Make a loaf and put in closed in a plastic wrap and allow it to rest on your work surface for 15-20 minutes

5. Slightly flour the surface use a rolling pin to roll out the dough beginning from the center. Use the rolling pin to roll the dough, roll as you lightly press on the upper right and left edges. Again, roll them out and continue the same operation until you get the thickness you desire. Allow it to dry for 10 minutes.

6. Use a little flour to sprinkle the dough and slightly fold the edges at the top and bottom, roll until it reaches at the center of the pasta circle and do it on both sides. Use a sharp knife to cut the strips 1 cm wide and unroll the strips.

7. Use the palm of your hand to roll the pappardelle a little at a time and put them on a lightly floured tray after forming a nest.

8. Cook and season them as preferred.

Lasagne

Prep time: 20 minutes

Serves: 6

Difficulty: 2

Ingredients:

- 4 eggs

- 1 pinch of salt

- 400 g 00 flour

Preparation:

1. Clean the work surface and make sure it is uncluttered and smooth.

2. In a classic fountain shape, pour in the flour and after you make a hole in the center, pour the shelled eggs inside and also add a pinch of salt. Use a fork to beat the eggs slowly and then move on to the more certainly and traditional method of using the fingers.

3. Incorporate the flour gradually on the edges until all ingredients are well mixed. When you get your egg pasta

ball, start working on it by occasionally beating it on the lightly floured pastry board and also vigorously massaging it. This phase should last for at least 15 minutes to 1 hour. Use a damp cloth to wrap the dough and allow it to rest for 30 minutes.

4. On a floured surface, take the dough again and massage it a little more. Begin pressing it with your hands as you roll it then to form a very thin sheet use the rolling pin, make a sheet less than a millimeter.

5. You can as well divide the dough into several portions that will be rolled out one at a given time. This will facilitate and ease this operation.

6. Depending on the size of the pan, you can now cut the pasta in rectangles of variable sizes or the shape of Lasagna. (The formats used most are 8x16 cm or 14x20)

7. You can now think about how to season the different layers after the sheet is ready.

ADVICE

You should massage and work on the dough for a long time in order to get elastic and smooth dough.

Try and avoid working from an environment, which is categorized with cold drafts.

Always add few tablespoons of warm water if you realize that the pasta excessively dries out.

Add 200 g of whisked, cooked and squeezed spinach to get green Lasagna.

Pici Fatti a Mano (Handmade Pici)

Prep time: 1 hour

Cook time: 10 minutes

Serves: 4

Difficulty: Medium

Cost: Very cheap

Ingredients:

- 270 ml warm water

- 2 tbsp olive oil

- 1 pinch of salt

- 450 g 00 flour

Preparation:

Hand-making

On a pastry board, use 450 g of flour and make a fountain. Pour about 270 ml and lukewarm water and also add salt. Add a tablespoon of oil and begin kneading. Use your hands to knead for a long time till you get a smooth, very firm and homogeneous dough. You can add small amounts of flour and water if necessary.

In planetary

In a bowl, add oil, salt and water, run at speed 2 and then add the flour, spoon after spoon until you obtain a paste that is consistent. When the pasta twists around the hook without almost or even adhering to it, just know it's ready. Start by using the spatula then the kneading hook.

How they are made (appiciatura)

1. Make the dough into a ball and put it in a plastic wrap. Let it rest for like 30 minutes after covering it with cloth. Knead it for like half a minute and take it back. On a floured surface, use a rolling pin to roll it to the thickness of 1 inch or even less. Use few oil drops to grease it and cut it into strips as large as they are high in a less or more square section.

2. Sprinkle a little wheat flour on the pastry board. Use a couple of handfuls of yellow or corn flour to prepare the tray and as you make the pici, it will help to dry them.

3. Use the fingers of your left hand to take the end of a strip and keep it raised slightly from the pastry board. Use the

palm of your right hand and roll it over by rubbing and use the left hand to stretch it by pulling gently. This will enable you get a long spaghetti which you will make of fairly and uniform fine diameter.

4. When done, for it to dry, throw it on the yellow surface and move it so that it sticks. You can repeat this for all the pasta. Make sure before you throw the pici in the tray, it has been well floured to avoid them from attacking each other. After you are done making all the pici, pass them on the pastry board. This should be after removing from the tray. Spread them out and separate them from each other but always flower them well with yellow flour.

5. Allow them to dry for at least 45 minutes and a maximum of 3 hours because when fully dry, they cook well. To avoid them touching the pastry board on the same side, move them occasionally. There is no problem in case they break while you move them, just attach together the ends that have broken and continue. Do not make them very long for the first few times. Two or three palms are okay.

Cooking

Use plenty of salted water to boil them for about 8 minutes. To avoid them sticking together, it's advisable to add a spoonful of oil in the cooking water. Gently take them and untie any agglomerates or knots that may have made them before cooking them. Throw them in boiling water in handfuls after freeing them from any excess flour.

ADVICE

For kneading, do not use hot or cold water. Use warm water. Use a large stove and boil them in much water because usually when they are thrown, they tend to lower the water temperature. When you boil them on a small stove or using little water, they will be sticky and will also take a long time to boil.

Once you remove them al dente, toss them in the pan with the sauce hot already, sauté or turn very little. Avoid adding cooking water so that they don't become sticky. The flour or the water or both should be measured when you make them. For each person, the dose that is normal is 1bout 65 g of water and 110 g of flour.

Not all flours absorb equally, so there could be small variations in the latter. To the initial dough, add an egg in the Montepulciano area using at least half a kilo of flour. With this, you get a more resistant and firmer paste.

Pasta Verde agli Spinaci (Green Pasta with Spinach)

Prep time: 60 minutes

Cook time: 10 minutes

Serves: 4

Difficulty: Medium

Cost: Low

Ingredients:

- 300 g 00 flour

- 3 medium eggs

- 60 g spinach

Preparation:

1. In making the green pasta with spinach, in a pan, put to boil 60 g of washed and drained spinach. Add a pinch of salt and water. Cover and allow them to cook and let the spinach dry and then pass it through a sieve to get a cream that is smooth.

2. Pour the sifter flour, the eggs that have been kept at room temperature and the spinach cream in a bowl and mix all the ingredients well.

3. Move to the pastry board and knead with your hands until you get homogeneous dough. If the dough is slightly hard or doesn't collect the flour completely, add 1 or 2 tablespoons of lukewarm water and keep kneading until the dough is compact and smooth and let it rests in a cool place covered for at least 30 minutes. Once the rest is done, the fresh pasta will be more elastic and softer. You can now prepare to roll it out and get the format you desire. You can use a machine or use the hands.

STORAGE

At the moment, we recommend using fresh egg pasta. If you want, you can keep it packed in vacuum for at most a couple of days.

Alternatively, once desired formats have you been made, it can be frozen raw.

Tagliatelle (Noodles)

Prep time: 30 minutes

Serves: 4

Difficulty: Medium

Ingredients

- 3 eggs at room temperature

- 300 g 00 flour

- Semolina to sprinkle

Preparation:

1. To prepare noodles, in a bowl, pour in the flour, make sure you remain with a little flour to add when necessary.

2. Create a basin and then break the eggs at room temperature in the center. Use a fork to beat the eggs and once they have absorbed some flour, keep kneading with a hand until you obtain a homogeneous mixture. On a lightly floured surface, keep kneading the dough for about 15 minutes until an elastic and smooth consistency is got.

3. Handle the glutinic mesh with energy but make sure you don't tear it. Make a ball and wrap it in a plastic wrap. Allow the dough to rest for 30 minutes at room temperature.

4. Divide the dough in 3 parts and then spread it easily. Flatten each part carefully after flouring it and keep other two parts in the film to avoid drying out.

5. Put the pasta machine on thickness mode for example maximum thickness and to obtain a first thick sheet, pass the dough through the rollers and to give a shape that is more regular, fold the two edges of the sheet towards the center and pass it between rollers again after flouring it lightly. Repeat this way until you get to the thickness you want.

6. Use a knife or tarot to level the dough obtained. This can be done on a floured pastry board to make the dough regular and in order to handle it easily, divide it into two parts. Using a thick machine, go over it again because you will have retired while working with it. Use a little semolina to sprinkle on both sides and leave the sheets to dry on each side for 5 minutes.

7. Fold a flap up to two thirds and take the sheet and begin rolling and create a flat roll. Cut the dough roll into slices of 7 mm thick while keeping the closure upwards.

8. From the ends, take the noodles on the hand and roll them around fingers in order to create a nest and let it to lay on a pastry board that is lightly floured. Continue the process until all the dough is finished. Now the noodles are ready, what remains is to cook them.

STORAGE

Raw noodles can be fee zed. To do so, on a tray, put the well-spaced nests of pasta and keep them in the freezer to harden for few hours. Once they harden, put them in frost bags and put them back in a freezer. Boil them directly from frozen in boiling water when you want to use them and then proceed per the recipe.

ADVICE

You can use a long rolling pin to roll out the fresh pasta if you prefer the traditional method. This will however take a lot of elbow grease and patience.

Fettuccine Fatte in Casa Ricetta della Nonna (Homemade Fettuccine Grandma's Recipe)

Prep time: 10 minutes

Serves: 5

Ingredients:

- 500 g 00 flour

- 5 whole eggs

- Salt

Preparation:

1. On a wooden worktop, arrange and make a classic fountain of flour by using your fingers to spread the central hole well. On a plate, break the eggs one by one and pour them in the fountain center and add a pinch of salt. It's advisable opt to break the eggs in the fountain directly. This is because you can run into a bad egg (This can be identified by the bad smells it gives once you have opened it. It is always recommended when making the dough with eggs;

break the eggs apart to avoid throwing away everything in case you find some eggs are spoilt.

2. When you have finished pouring the eggs in the fountain and seasoning them with salt, use a fork to gently beat them and add flour as you beat the eggs. This helps because it doesn't let the egg to run down for all sides. Another way that could be faster, use your hands to collect all the flour. Begin working with the mixture while kneading in order to get dry, smooth and not too soft dough.

3. Wrap the dough in a plastic wrap and allow it to rest for about 30 minutes. Meanwhile, start preparing the dressing for your homemade fettuccine.

4. Take the dough again after 30 minutes and on a wooden board, sprinkle a little flour. Use your hands to crust the dough a little to make a round pizza then use a rolling pin to begin rolling out. Cut the dough into two and make two sheets if you find it more comfortable to work using less dough.

5. As you use the rolling pin to roll out the dough while pulling and rubbing your palms on it, bringing them closer and also moving them away, put it on the table. Keep using the rolling pin to pull it and roll it up and also continue

rubbing with your hands until you obtain a sheet of about 1 or 2 millimeters.

6. When you get the desired sheet, spread it on the table and allow it dry for few minutes. Sprinkle with little flour and begin rolling up. Begin cutting the sheet into the sizes you want, using a sharp knife. From 5 to 6 millimeters for pappardelle and from 3 to 4 millimeters for tagliatelle and fettuccine.

7. Spread a large tablecloth or dishcloth once sliced, use your hands to spread the rolls and to unroll the fettuccine and arrange them, sprinkling a little flour on the dishcloth. Put a pan of water to boil to cook them while they are covered with a table or dish cloth.

8. Pour the fettuccine in the water once it boils and cook for 6 minutes. Serve and enjoy your meal.

Chapter 5: Short Pasta Recipes

Orecchiette

Prep time: 60 minutes

Serves: 6

Difficulty: Medium

Cost: Very low

Ingredients:

- 400 g durum wheat semolina

- 200 g lukewarm water

- ¼ tsp. salt

Preparation:

1. Pour the wheat flour on a pastry board

2. Create a fountain

3. Season with salt

4. Pour water at the middle and incorporate the flour using your fingers. Do a little at a time the water to be absorbed by the flour.

5. Use your hands to knead to form an elastic and homogeneous consistency. This takes approximately 10 minutes. Shape the dough into a circular shape and use a cloth to cover it. Rest for 15-20 minutes at room temperature.

6. After resting, cut a piece using a pastry cutter and leave the rest covered. Make a loaf whose thickness is about 1 cm. From the loaf, form smaller 1 cm pieces.

7. Use a blade knife that is smooth to form small shells on every piece. This is done by dragging the pieces on the pastry board, which is lightly floured towards you. Form the orecchiette by turning over the shell on itself. Repeat the process until the dough is finished and by the end you will have your Apulian orecchiette.

STORAGE

Use a cloth to dry the covered orecchiette. Store for about four weeks.

You can as well freeze them on a tray and when stiff, move to frost bags.

ADVICE

When cooking the orecchiette, do so in salted boiling water for 6 minutes. Use turnip greens to season them. You can also use a tomato sauce!

Farfalle

Prep time: 40 minutes

Cook time: 5 minutes

Serves: 4

Difficulty: Difficult

Cost: Low

Ingredients:

- 200 g 00 flour

- 2 medium Eggs

Preparation:

1. For the butterflies, you begin by putting the flour on a weighing scale, keep on adding it on the pastry board (leave some flour behind to add just in case the dough is too soft). Form a bowl at the middle and add the eggs. Start with a fork to mix, and then proceed using your hand. Knead until the dough is elastic and smooth consistently.

2. Form the dough into a sphere and cover it using a transparent film. Allow a minimum of 20 minutes for the pasta to rest.

3. After 20 minutes, divide the dough into quarters. Get one piece and place it in the pasta machine (leave the rest covered in a plastic wrap). Work on the dough until it is 1 mm thick.

4. Use a pastry cutter and make rectangular shapes on the sheets you got and with the notched part, form vertical strips with a width of 7 cm. With the smooth part, cut horizontally into 4 cm. Use your forefinger and thumb and to form butterflies. Lift a piece of dough at the rectangle's center using your thumb. You will create another fold at the middle; bring the other flap to the center using your index finger creating another fold.

5. Tighten the middle to fix the butterflies' shape; repeat for the remaining dough and put them on a tray.

6. While making the butterflies, lightly flour a tray and arrange them. Allow about 30 minutes to dry. Cook the butterflies in boiling water that is salted.

STORAGE

Put the dry pasta farfalle in frost bags and put in a freezer up to a month.

ADVICE

Use fresh spinach pasta to get green farfalle!

Cavatelli

Prep time: 15 minutes

Cook time: 10 minutes

Serves: 4

Difficulty: Difficult

Cost: Very Low

Ingredients:

- 125 g Durum wheat semolina

- 125 g 00 flour

- 130 g Water

- 1 tbsp Extra virgin olive oil

Preparation:

1. Mix the Durum wheat semolina and 00 flour in a bowl and move them to a pastry board to form a fountain at the middle. Mix by adding little water.

2. Add oil and keep on kneading to get soft and smooth dough and make it round.

3. Cover the pasta using a film and allow about 13 minutes to rest (this makes the dough elastic). Take a piece of pasta and form a tube. Divide it into pieces with a width of 1 cm.

4. To form the cavatelli, dig inside using some little pressure and curl the edges. Put it on a tray and drizzle the semolina over. Allow 2 hours for cavatelli to dry for it to be consistent when you cook (you can also cook immediately but it is advised against).

5. Add to salted boiling water and cook for about 8-10 minutes while constantly checking.

STORAGE

Refrigerate the cavatelli for up to 4 days. You can freeze the cavatelli for 30 minutes to avoid them sticking together.

You can store the dry cavatelli for up to 2 weeks.

ADVICE

More cooking time is needed as pasta dries. Therefore, you need to taste the cavatelli to check the cooking.

Strozzapreti Emiliani Fatti in Casa

(Homemade Emilian Strozzapreti)

Prep time: 30 minutes

Cook time: 5 minutes

Serves: 4

Difficulty: Medium

Cost: Low

Ingredients:

- 500 ml water

- 1 kg 00 flour

- ½ tsp. Salt

Preparation:

1. Mix 00 flour with salt and add water little by little as you mix with your hand. Keep kneading to until thoroughly mixed.

2. Move the dough to a working surface and knead to form homogeneous and smooth dough. Use a plastic wrap to cover and allow 30 minutes to rest.

3. In the meantime, cut the dough into two and leave one part covered. Roll the dough to about 1 mm thickness. Use a toothless blade knife to cut, and then use the tip of the knife to remove the strips to avoid sticking.

4. Use a cutter to cut 2 cm strips. For every strip, roll it starting from one end to form clams of at least 3 cm. Repeat the process until dough is finished.

5. Put the Strozzapreti trays that are floured lightly and keep it in the freezer until you are ready to use it.

Strascinati Fatti in Casa (Homemade Strascinati)

Prep time: 30 minutes

Serves: 4

Difficulty: Easy

Cost: Low

Ingredients:

- 200 ml water

- Salt

- 400 g durum wheat flour

Preparation:

1. Knead the mentioned ingredients until you get a hard and homogeneous mixture. If you want, you can use a machine for this process and then remove the mixture from the basket immediately you finish the mixing phase.

2. Use the mixture to make a ball and wrap it in a plastic wrap. Allow it to rest for 30 minutes. Divide the dough in many parts and using a lightly floured surface, work on every part

of the dough and make a long stick that has a diameter of 8 mm and cut them into pieces. This cut can be made approximately every 4-5 cm.

3. Press each piece of the dough and make the movement from top to the bottom using the three central fingers. Work on all the pasta that is available in this way and take care not to move the Strascinati that has been worked on, on a slightly and lightly floured spaced self to avoid them sticking together.

4. Allow them to dry for 30 minutes. After this, it's now possible to cook your homemade Strascinati.

Gnocchi di Patate (Potato Gnocchi)

Prep time: 20 minutes

Cook time: 40 minutes

Serves: 4

Difficulty: Easy

Cost: Very low

Ingredients:

- 1 medium egg

- 300 g 00 flour

- 1 kg potatoes

- Salt to taste

For the version without eggs:

- 350 g 00 flour

- 15 g salt

- 1 kg potatoes

Preparation:

1. In preparing this recipe, begin by pouring the flour on a pastry board and the boiling the potatoes. In a large pot, put the potatoes and cover them with much cold water.

2. When the water is boiling, depending on their size, count like 35 minutes. Use a fork to test. When the prongs enter the middle with little effort, know they are ready and drain them.

3. While still hot, peel and crush them immediately on the flour and then add the beaten egg and salt together and use your hands to mix them till you get compact but soft dough.

4. Don't forget that if you work on them a lot, the gnocchi will be hard while cooking and only knead the dough. Use your fingertips to roll out a piece of the dough to get the bigoli; the loves 2cm thick and for this, you should occasionally use semolina flour to dust the pastry board. To prevent the remaining dough from drying out, cover it with a tea towel.

5. Cut the loaves into chunks and to get a classic shape, drag on the gnocchi row by using your thumb to lightly press them. A fork can be used to drag them on prongs if you do

not have the gnocchi row and to avoid sticking, use semolina flour.

6. Lightly flour a dish towel and set it on a tray. Arrange the gnocchi on a tray, keeping space from one to the other.

7. To cook them, bring salted water to boil and pour them in and cook until they come to the surface. Season and drain and then serve.

For the version without eggs

1. While the potatoes are still hot, mash them on the pastry board using a potato masher. Add flour and salt and then use your hands to knead in order to get a compact but soft mixture.

2. Pick up a dough portion at a time and roll it using the tips of the fingers in order to form the loaves of 2 cm thickness. Cut the loaves in 5 pieces and pass every dough piece on the prongs of a fork or on a gnocchi row with the use of the thumb to lightly press.

3. Cook the dumplings eggless in much boiling salted water and as soon as they come to the surface, drain them.

STORAGE

You can keep the potato gnocchi raw by leaving it for a couple of hours on the cloth. But since they will have dried in the air, the cooking might be a bit longer.

Dumplings can also be freezing. For this, put the tray in a freezer for 20 minutes and put the potato dumplings in a food bag, and keep doing so until all of them have been frozen.

Just throw them in boiling salted water if you want to cook them, without defrosting them first.

ADVICE

If you desire making your potato gnocchi more special, use ingredients for coloring that is for a yellowish color, use turmeric or for red gnocchi with bacon pesto and marjoram, use a hint of tomato concentrate. Whichever color the past is, whether yellow, red or white, it doesn't really matter. What's important is that they aren't new potatoes because these contain much water. It's advisable to use aged potatoes because they are poor in water and rich in starch and to be kneaded, they require less flour.

Garganelli all'Uovo Fatti in Casa (Homemade Egg Garganelli)

Prep time: 60 minutes

Serves: 8

Difficulty: Medium

Cost: Low

Ingredients:

- 100 g durum wheat semolina

- 250 g 00 flour

- Water

- Re-milled semolina for dusting

- 3 eggs

- 2 tbsp. extra virgin olive oil

- Salt to taste

Preparation:

For homemade egg Garganelli you can proceed in two ways:

1. Homemade egg Garganelli first way:

- Make the dough for the garganelli by hand: sift the flours and pour them on a pastry board. Make a hole in the center, where you will break the eggs, add the salt and extra virgin olive oil.

- Start by beating the eggs with a fork, and slowly taking some flour. Then continue to knead with your hands, add a little water (just enough) to obtain a workable dough, but not too soft. Knead until it is smooth and elastic. It will take about 10 minutes. Wrap the dough with plastic wrap and let it rest for at least 1/2 hour.

- After resting, cut the dough in half. The part you don't use right away, keep it wrapped in cling film, and then roll it out later.

- Roll out the dough with a rolling pin, until you get a thin sheet.

- With a wheel cut the dough so as to obtain many squares of about 4 cm each side. Cover them with cling film to keep them from drying out.

- Take one square of pasta at a time, and with the help of the wooden stick, roll it up on itself, starting from the corner. Turn it by pressing lightly on the pastry board, so that the pasta closes well. Pass it on the rigagnocchi. If you have the special tool for garganelli you can train it directly above.

- Remove the garganello from the stick and place it on a dripping pan lined with parchment paper. Proceed in the same way to make all the garganelli.

- You can cook them immediately, or you can keep them for a few days, simply covered with a clean cloth.

2. Homemade egg Garganelli second way

- Make the dough for the Garganelli with the machine: put all the ingredients in the planetary mixer (with the hook) or food processor, and let it go until the dough becomes a smooth and elastic ball.

- Wrap it with plastic wrap and let it rest. Then cut some not too big pieces and pass them several times through the rolls of the pasta machine. Keep on tapering it more and more, increasing or increasing the number, until you reach 5, or better yet 6.

- Then proceed in the same way as to make the garganelli by hand.

Busiate Trapanesi (Busiate from Trapani)

Prep time: 1 hour

Cook time: 5 minutes

Serves: 10

Difficulty: Low

Cost: Very cheap

Ingredients

- 400 ml water

- 2 tbsp. extra virgin olive oil

- 1 kg Durum wheat semolina

- 2 tsp. salt

Preparation:

1. On the wooden pastry board, pour the semolina, in the center, make a bowl and put some little water, oil and salt.

2. Begin kneading by slowly adding the water that is needed. Knead until an elastic and smooth mixture has been obtained. Leave to rest for 1 hour.

3. When you use the planetary mixer, put all ingredients apart from water that is required to be poured slowly slowly. Working on the dough by the planetary mixer takes about 10 minutes for one to get a great result of pasta.

4. It's now time to make the Busiate. Make small rolls from the cut small pasta pieces like thin breadsticks and cut them 10 cm long. Diagonally putting the wooden skewer over the roll end, twist the dough around it and form a curl. By sliding out, remove the Busiate and keep using all the pasta.

Maltagliati

Prep time: 1 hour

Cook time: 2 minutes

Serves: 4

Difficulty: Medium

Cost: Low

Ingredients

- All-purpose flour

- Sea salt

- Water

Preparation:

To make the pasta

1. Use the All-purpose flour to dust the baking sheets.

2. Mix the flour and salt and add water. Use your hands to combine to form dough. Pass the dough through the pasta machine on the widest setting. Use a knife to cut if it becomes very long.

3. Alternatively, you can use a rolling pin to press and make the dough thin.

4. Using a knife cut out your dough into 6-by-4-inch sheets.

5. Dust the pasta sheets with flour and let them rest for 5 minutes so they are not too sticky.

6. Put them one on top of the other (maximum three sheets) and, using a sharp knife, cut the pasta sheets into 1½- to 2-inch irregular shapes resembling a rhombus.

7. Separate the cut pasta and transfer to the baking sheets.

8. Repeat the process until all dough is finished.

Cooking the pasta

1. Bring salted water to boil in a large saucepan. Cook the pasta until al dente, or for 3 minutes. Take a bite to test this.

2. After 3 minutes, use a slotted spoon to remove the pasta and remove the excess water by shaking gently.

3. Serve immediately with the sauce of your choice.

You can use tools and equipment like, Pasta machine or rolling pin, Knife, no serrated, 3 baking sheets, Large pot, Wooden spoon, Slotted spoon

STORAGE

Maltagliati can also be frozen raw. For freezing, put the tray with the Maltagliati in a freezer to harden for some hours. Put them in frost bags when they are well hardened, its better if they are already portioned and return then in the freezer.

When you need to use them, directly boil them from frozen in the boiling water and proceed per the recipe.

Chapter 6: Stuffed Pasta Recipes

Ravioli del Plin

Prep time: 2 hours

Cook time: 1 hour 30 minutes

Serves: 8

Difficulty: Medium

Cost: Medium

Ingredients:

- 4 eggs

- 400 g flour

For the stuffing:

- 1 large onion

- 1 egg

- 30 g spinach

- 200 g pork loin

- 200 g rabbit legs

- 300 g carrots

- 250 g calf pulp

- 100 g celery

- 30 g escarole

- Vegetable broth

- Extra virgin olive oil

- 15 g parmesan cheese

- Salt

- Pepper to taste

Preparation:

1. Put the flour on the work surface and break the eggs inside, one at a time. Mix the eggs using a spoon, starting form the inside. Knead the dough using a fork or with your hands and mix all the flour. If the dough is a bit hard, add few tablespoons of water and continue kneading until its compact and smooth.

2. Using a cling film, cover the pasta and leave it to rest in a cool and dry place for an hour.

3. Cut celery, onions and carrots and set them aside. Remove the veal pulp and the fat part of the loin. You can as well ask the butcher to clean the meat for you by removing the parts that have fats.

4. Heat a few tablespoons of oil in a large saucepan and fry the veal pulp and pork loin until golden brown. Add 2 tablespoons of oil in another pan and fry the rabbit eggs till they are brown.

5. When they are well browned, add the meat, celery, carrots, onions, pepper and salt in a single pan and add water or a ladle of broth. Cover them and cook for 1 hour. If it's necessary, add water or broth during the cooking process.

6. When the meat is ready, remove and let it cool. Keep the cooking juices with the vegetables aside for use in dressing the ravioli. Meanwhile, in a separate pan, add some oil and cook the escarole and spinach until they are wilted. This takes about 5 minutes. If you want, you can cook the endive and spinach in a single pan but first cook the endive for few minutes and add the spinach later since it takes less time.

7. In the meantime, cut the veal meat, pork loin and bone the rabbit into pieces and put all the meats in a mixer. Cut them and add the vegetables, cheese and the egg. Season it with pepper and salt and if it is necessary, add a little broth.

8. Blend all the ingredients together till you get a very compact and dense filling.

9. Now start preparing the ravioli del plin. Take some dough and roll out the thin sheet. On half of the bottom sheet, put half a ball of filling about 20 g and between them, leave a space of 1-2 cm. Quickly work on the dough to avoid it from hardening.

10. Fold the pasta on itself and pinch the edges of the dough on the sides with the fingers, from the long side. Cut the pasta lengthwise few millimeters from the filling using a wheel cut and then separate the ravioli and give it a rectangular shape.

11. Get a tray with a cloth dusted with flour and put the ravioli. Take the previously stewed vegetables and place them in a mixer and blend them till you get a homogeneous and smooth sauce.

12. In abundant salted water, cook the ravioli del plin for few minutes. Drain and season with the sauce obtained from the cooking surface of the meat as soon as they rise to the surface.

13. Serve and enjoy your ravioli del plin.

STORAGE

You can keep the cooked and seasoned plin ravioli in an emetic container in the refrigerator for about 2 days.

You can as well freeze them when they are putting them on a tray that is well-spaced to avoid sticking and you can transfer them to a food bag once they are frozen.

You can cook the plin while its still frozen. Cook them in abundant salted water frozen till they rise to the surface.

If the meat is fresh, the filling can also be frozen.

ADVICE

This is a good dish. You can test it with a sage dressing or classic butter.

If you are following this recipe and the sauce that is roast turns us too liquid, don't worry; let it dry for few minutes on the fire.

Cappelletti

Prep time: 60 minutes

Cook time: 20 minutes

Serves: 6

Difficulty: Medium

Cost: Medium

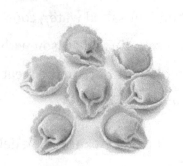

Ingredients:

For egg pasta:

- 4 eggs

- 400 g 00 flour

For the stuffing:

- 50 g celery

- 60 g carrots

- 150 g pork, minced

- 50 g Parmigiano Reggiano, grated

- 50 g red wine

- 30 g extra virgin olive oil

- 100 g chicken breast

- 100 g veal, minced

- 1 egg

- 60 g golden onions

- Nutmeg

- Black pepper

- Salt

Preparation:

1. Start by preparing the egg pasta. In a large bowl, pour the flour, add the lightly beaten eggs and flour.

2. Use your hands to knead until you get homogeneous and smooth dough, which you will leave to rest at room temperature after wrapping it in a plastic bag for 30 minutes.

3. Meanwhile, be preparing the filling. Cut the carrots, celery and onions and pour in a large pan with oil. Let it stew for like 10 minutes while oftenly stirring.

4. Cut the chicken into tubes and use a knife to chop finely and then add the initial stir-fry with the minced pork and veal.

5. Use a wooden spoon to stir for 6 minutes and then blend with red wine.

6. Once the alcohol evaporates, add the pepper and salt and cook for 4-5 minutes. Pour the meat that is cooked in the mixer and get a mixture that is finer.

7. Transfer the lightly beaten egg and the grated parmesan into a container. Add ground black pepper, salt and nutmeg and then mix. Keep aside.

8. Remove the film and roll out with a rolling pin or a pasta machine after taking the egg pasta. Roll on a lightly floured pastry board. Slightly flatten the dough, flour it lightly and put it between two rollers if you are using a pasta machine.

9. It is crucial to always begin from the widest thickness till you get to the narrow one adding a pinch of flour on each side each time. During this operation, sometimes the dough

deforms and you have to fold it by pulling one flap then the other towards the center.

10. Finally, slightly squeeze in the middle and begin pulling the dough between the rollers again. Get thin sheets of about 0.6 mm and cover them with plastic wraps to avoid drying out as a result of much air

11. Then cut 5 cm squares of dough with a 24 smooth wheel that you will fill with a teaspoon of compound. Try to position the seasoning well by compacting it in the center and fold the opposite end and form a triangle. Pull the two ends towards you and join them.

12. Flatten down and join them slightly pinching with your fingers. Since they tend to open while you are cooking, make sure they are closed tightly. Repeat this operation for all the others until you get all the cappelletti ready to be cooked.

13. While you prepare them, lay them on a tray where you will have put a lightly floured dish and clean cloth with semolina.

STORAGE

If you have used fresh ingredients, cappelletti can be frozen. Just place them on a tray while they are kept apart, put the tray in a freezer for about 30 minutes.

Once they have hardened very well, but it's better if they are portioned already, put them in frost bags and take them back to the freezer.

When you need to use them, directly boil them from frozen in boiling water and continue as per the recipe.

ADVICE

During processing, if the dough gets so dry, you can use water to brush the surface of pasta disks.

You can replace the 3 types of minced meat with what you prefer.

Caramelle Ricotta e Spinaci (Ricotta and Spinach Candies)

Prep time: 90 minutes

Cook time: 20 minutes

Serves: 4

Difficulty: Easy

Cost: Low

Ingredients:

For egg pasta:

- 2 eggs

- 250 g 00 flour

- 1 yolk

For the stuffing:

- 1 pinch, nutmeg

- 250 g spinach

- 50 g Parmigiano Reggiano

- 125 g cow's milk ricotta

- Black pepper

- Salt

For the dressing

- Parmesan cheese

- 6 leaves, sage

- 100 g butter

Preparation:

1. Preparing the ricotta and spinach candies, you start with egg pasta. In a bowl, pour the flour and keep about 50 g to add if need be, add eggs and do everything inside one bowl. Once the eggs are absorbed, continue handling the dough on a work surface until its elastic and smooth.

2. Give it a spherical shape once they are ready and let them rest in a cook place with lights on for 30 minutes after wrapping them in a plastic wrap.

3. To prepare the filling, in a non-stick pan, put very little salt water, boil the spinach or simply sauté them on low heat or cook them in the steam. Squeeze and chop them finely. The spinach will weigh 100 gr once cooked and well squeezed.

4. In a bowl, put the chopped spinach in which you will add the parmesan and ricotta, salt, pepper and nutmeg. Use a soft but compact mixture to mix all the ingredients.

5. In a very thin sheet, roll out the egg pasta which you will cut into rectangles measuring 10x8 cm. Put a little teaspoon of filling in every rectangle of pasta and on a longer side, wrap the dough on itself.

6. Model your sweets by turning the left flap counterclockwise and the right flap clockwise as though to close the paper of the candy. Using a serrated wheel cut the outer edges of both edges.

7. After modeling all the candies, put them to dry on a floured work surface for an hour. In salted boiling water, cook the pasta for at least 5 minutes.

8. Let the sage leaves gild in melted butter in a pan.

9. Drain the candies once cooked and season them with sage and butter and grated parmesan to taste.

10. Your spinach and ricotta candies are ready to be served.

STORAGE

Ricotta and spinach candies can be kept in a refrigerator for one day.

You can alternatively freeze them raw. To freeze, put the candies on the tray in the freezer for them to harden for some hours. Put them in frost bags once they are well hardened and take them back to the freezer.

If you need to use them, directly boil them from frozen in boiling water per the recipe.

ADVICE

Pack the candies as soon as you pull the dough when it's still workable and wet since it tends to quickly dry out otherwise it will make the filling to leak out because it will break in the twisting process.

Casoncelli

Prep time: 60 minutes

Serves: 6

Difficulty: Medium

Cost: Medium

Ingredients:

For egg pasta:

- 165 g medium, eggs

- 300 g 00 flour

For the stuffing:

- 150 g, Veal, ground

- 150 g Pork, ground

- 20 g Parmigiano Reggiano, grated

- 150 g Chard

- 15 g Macaroons

- 10 g Extra virgin olive oil

- 30 g Breadcrumbs

- 20 g Raisins

- 3 g Parsley

Preparation:

1. Begin by preparing the fresh egg pasta to make the casoncelli. In a large bowl, put the flour and keep aside like 50 g to add if needed basing on how much the eggs absorb.

2. Pout the slightly beaten eggs in the hole with a classic fountain shape that you made in the center.

3. Begin using your hands to knead. Fist in a bowl and when the dough is consistent, transfer to the pastry board. Continue kneading vigorously until you get quite elastic and firm dough.

4. Form a ball and line it with a cling film and let it rest for 30 minutes at room temperature. After this, it will be easier to spread and more elastic.

5. Meanwhile, start filling. Rinse the raisins under running water and for them to soften soak them in hot water for about 10 minutes. In the meantime, wash the beets, check the stem base and cut the leaves roughly. In the bottom of

the pan, heat a little oil and put the beets to stew. On low heat, allow them to dry. This takes few minutes.

6. Put the minced pork and beef in a glass mixer and add the breadcrumbs, Grana, the cooked chard and the whole amaretti and operate the blades by chopping until you get a fine compound. Add the grated parsley and lemon zest and lastly the well-drained and softened raisins.

7. Do the seasoning with pepper and salt and mix to obtain a homogeneous mixture, which can be transferred to a sac-a-poche. Recover the rested egg pasta, divide it into smaller loaves and with the help of the knuckle, roll the dough until you get 1 mm thick sheets. To get about 21 cm wide strips, cut the sheet length wise.

8. To keep them well-spaced from each other with the sac-a-poche distributed along the strip of the walnuts that are stuffed, using s damp brush or by sprinkling, wet the pasta with water around the stuffing to make it more adhesive. Fold the upper edge of the strip after collecting it, over the stuffing nuts and wit finer pressure, make them adhere and so that the bubbles don't form inside your casoncelli, make sure that you let the air escape.

9. Equipping yourself with a 6 cm diameter festooned pastry ring and to ensure the shape of a crescent, keep half of it out and to form your ravioli, cop pate. Use a little water to moist them and pinch the ravioli with the filling. Fold them towards the semicircle edge.

10. Adhere to the moistened dough to form the casoncelli by exerting slight pressure. Continue like this until both the filling and the dough are exhausted and when they are ready, let the casoncelli rest on a floured tray before cooking for 25-30 minutes.

11. Cook the casoncelli in salted boiling water for 6 minutes. Season as you like one its drained.

STORAGE

Casoncelli can be kept in an airtight container in a fridge for a maximum of 2 days.

You can freeze them while raw for at least a month and you can directly cook them in boiling water without thawing them first.

ADVICE

casoncelli can be seasoned by skipping in a pan after cooking them with sage, butter and diced bacon.

Mezzelune al Salmone ed Erba Cipollina (Salmon and Chives Mezzelune)

Prep time: 60 minutes

Cook time: 6 minutes

Serves: 4

Difficulty: Medium

Cost: Medium

Ingredients:

400 g Pasta, fresh (the recipe is at the beginning of the book)

For the filling:

- 2 tbsps. Chives

- 400 g Cow's milk ricotta

- 300 g Salmon, smoked

- Salt

- Pepper

For the dressing:

- 2 tbsp. Chives

- 100 g butter

Preparation

1. Prepare the egg pasta per the recipe.

2. Use a knife to chop the salmon, put in a bowl and add 2 tablespoons of chopped chives, little freshly ground pepper and ricotta and add salt. Adjust if necessary.

3. Use a pasta machine or by hand, roll the egg pasta and form a sheet as thin as possible and make discs with a diameter of at least 5 cm with the help of a round pastry cutter.

4. On each disc, put a little filling and form a crescent by closing it on yourself and to weld the edges, lightly press them. Moist the edges with water if the paste doesn't stick well when using a brush.

5. In pan with much salted water, cook the crescents and also melt the butter in a pan.

6. Drain the crescents and sprinkle with chopped chives and season them with melted butter.

7. Serve the salmon crescents while hot.

ADVICE

You can season the crescents with cream, a light and fluid bechamel sauce that is flavored with chives or with salmon.

Tortellini

Prep time: 150 minutes

Cook time: 10 minutes

Serves: 6

Difficulty: Medium

Cost: Medium

Ingredients:

For egg pasta:

- 400g 00 flour

- 4 eggs

For the stuffing:

- 70 g Pork loin

- 80 g Parma raw ham

- 70 g Beef veal pulp

- 150 g Parmesan cheese to be grated

- 1 large egg

- 80 g Bologna Mortadella

- 20 g Butter

- Nutmeg

- Black pepper to taste

- Salt to taste

Preparation:

1. In preparing the tortellini, begin with preparing the egg pasta. Add the flour on a pastry board and form a hole at the middle and then add the eggs. Use a fork to break eggs and start incorporating. Switch to using your hands and keep kneading to get a smooth and soft dough. Use a cling film to cover and allow a minimum of 30 minutes to rest.

2. Meanwhile get the filling ready: cut the pork loin and veal meat in coarse pieces and place the aside. Repeat with mortadella and raw ham.

3. Add butter to a pan and melt it and add the meat. Cook it for 10 minutes until it is brown. Allow it to cool and add the

meat, mortadella and raw ham to a mixer. Blend until well mixed. Add pepper, nutmeg, parmesan and egg and blend further to form a dough. Place the pasta in a pasta machine and roll it out into a thin sheet; you can alternatively use a rolling pin.

4. Cut 4cm thick squares from the dough using a sharp knife or cutter wheel. Ensure the remaining pasta is always covered. Put some few grams of the filling and make the tortellini. Fold a square to a triangular shape and press edges to stick them.

5. Fold the triangle's base upwards. Rest the resulting dough on your index finger, the triangle tip looking up. Join together the ends using some pressure and turn them down to make the edges fit.

6. Lay the tortellini on cloth that is floured lightly. Repeat till all ingredients are finished. Place the tortellini in a cloth that is floured and you can proceed to cooing in meat broth.

STORAGE

Freeze each tortellini while separated for half an hour. Put them together and freeze.

Allow them to dry if you cannot freeze them. Put them in a closed in a container and put in a fridge, either cooked or raw.

ADVICE

Cook the tortellini strictly in meat broth and serve with the broth.

You can use the meat that you prefer e.g. pork, turkey, or chicken.

Ravioli di Ricotta (Ricotta Ravioli)

Prep time: 60
minutes

Serves: 24

Difficulty: Medium

Cost: Low

Ingredients:

For egg pasta:

- 2 large eggs

- 250 g 00 flour

- 1 yolk

- Durum wheat semolina

For the stuffing:

- 20 g Grana Padano to be grated

- 400 g Cows milk ricotta

- Nutmeg to taste

- Black pepper

- Salt to taste

Preparation:

1. You begin by preparing the egg pasta. Add flour to a bowl and add the eggs. Vigorously knead the ingredients to form a smooth and homogenous mixture. Add flour if need be. You can also add some water, little by little, if it is too dry.

2. Move the dough to a flour-dusted work surface and use a cling film to cover the dough. Allow about 30 minutes to rest at room temperature.

3. Meanwhile you can be filling as the dough rests. Get a bowl and season with pepper and salt. Add thyme leaves, combine with the ricotta.

4. Move the mixture into a sac-à-poche and refrigerate. The pasta will have rested enough. Divide it into equal halves. Take one half and leave the other one covered. Use re-milled semolina flour to flour the first half of the dough and roll it through the pasta machine in the widest setting to get a 2mm-thick sheet. Place the sheet on a flour-dusted work

surface. Repeat with the remaining dough. Create rectangular pieces and arrange them 3cm apart.

5. Drizzle water on the sheet's edges or use a kitchen brush to brush with ravioli. Match the edges and press them together using your fingers to remove air.

6. Use a notched cutter wheel or a sharp knife to make the ravioli starting at filling to another, 4x4 cm. Flour a tray and arrange the ravioli there. The ravioli is now ready for cooking.

STORAGE

You can freeze the ricotta ravioli up to a maximum of one month. Harden the ravioli by placing them while still on a tray in a freezer for two hours. Set them in frost bags and return them to a freezer.

ADVICE

You can use other herbs such as dill or parsley to personalize the filling.

Tortelli di Zucca (Pumpkin Tortelli)

Prep time: 150 minutes

Cook time: 20 minutes

Serves: 4

Difficulty: Difficult

Cost: Medium

Ingredients:

For egg pasta:

- 104 g eggs

- 200 g 00 flour

For the stuffing:

- 160 g Macaroons

- 170 g Pear valance mustard

- 52 g eggs

- 500 g pumpkin

- 65 g Parmigiano Reggiano, grated

- Salt to taste

- Nutmeg to be grated

Preparation:

1. Prepare the filling and put it in the fridge to rest overnight for a flavorful mix. Cut the pumpkin into slices and put them on a parchment-lined pan.

2. Bake for 20 minutes at 220° in a preheated oven, while occasionally pricking using a fork. The result should be a soft pumpkin. Add the amaretti in a bowl as the pumpkin cooks and use your hands to crumble them.

3. Use a knife to chop the pear valance mustard. When the pumpkin is ready, rest it in the oven to cool. This also allows it to dry and loose water. Use a spoon to scoop the pulp and add it into a potato masher and set a small bowl to collect.

4. Add the amaretti and the mustard to the pulp and use a spatula to mix.

5. Add in cheese and egg and thoroughly mix. Add salt and the nutmeg. Use a plastic wrap to cover and refrigerate it overnight, or 24 hours.

6. Prepare the pasta: pour the flour on pastry board and scoop a well at the middle. Break in the egg and use a fork to incorporate. Switch to using hands and mix to get smooth and soft dough. Add water if the dough is too dry and if it is too sticky, add some flour. Do this until you obtain smooth dough. Form the dough into a spherical shape. Use a cling film to cover the dough.

7. Allow a minimum of 30 minutes for the dough to rest at room temperature. After the time has elapsed, divide the dough into two. Leave one half covered in the cling film and put the other through the pasta machine or using a rolling pin. Roll the dough to get 1mm thick rectangles.

8. Dust a work surface with flour and roll the dough on top. Use a pastry cutter to level the dough and get strips of 9cm width. Put the strip on the filling piles in the top part while you space the piles, on the pasta strip. Cover the filling by folding the pasta strip: brush the pastry with water if it is a bit dry.

9. Use a wheel cutter to cut shape and size you desire. The tortelli size and shape vary depending on traditions and one's personal preference. Proceed till all pasta is finished. If you wish, you can cook, as your tortelli is ready.

STORAGE

Freeze the tortelli and when it becomes hard, put in a frost bag and put it back in a freezer for storage.

ADVICE

For filling that is less sweet, use mature cheese or you can add more salt to balance. You can use sage and butter to season your tortelli as this combo enhances the filling flavor. You can have it with a tomato sauce or a sausage ragout if you want a taste that is decisive. You can as well bring in cooked seasonal vegetables to get a unique dish.

147

CONCLUSION

The art of making pasta has a history of hundreds of years, do not expect to make masterpieces at the first attempt but continue to practice cooking even more delicious pasta dishes

The art of making pasta has a history of hundreds of years, do not expect to make masterpieces at the first attempt but continue to practice cooking even more delicious pasta dishes

When walking through the refrigerator case of the grocery store, you might see one of those clear plastic cases of pasta that is labeled as being "Fresh" and be tempted to grab it. The reality is these shouldn't be called fresh pasta. It's just that "Premade soft pasta product" doesn't exactly roll off the tongue.

Most of the time, these prepackaged versions are made with dough stabilizers and other additives to help them keep longer in grocery store cases. Many of these additives keep the pasta from interacting with the sauce. The pasta tends to slide around in the sauce like two strangers instead of forming a harmonious relationship with it.

The price for these packages of premade pasta is usually very high when compared to the cheap price of rolling out fresh pasta made from flour and eggs at home.

Fresh pasta made at home and often finished in the sauce has the ability to form a relationship with the sauce in a way that benefits both components. The process is actually rather easy once you understand the principles of making and rolling it out. All at the cost of around a dollar!

This homemade pasta cookbook seeks to rekindle an art that has been practiced by mankind for many centuries, but with the advent of modernization, this art is slowly losing its shine and place in our modern kitchens and culinary practice.

There are a lot of different kinds of pasta around the world and exist many ways of its cooking and preparing. This cookbook features pasta dough illustrating the ease of making the dough and the ingredients you would require making the dough.

The cookbook also highlights stuffed, short and long pastas with amazing results.

After the pastas are cooked and ready to be enjoyed, it is important to understand how best to enjoy the meal.

Pasta dishes as alluded to earlier are indeed dishes that are enjoyed widely across different regions of the world and on many dining tables in homes across the world.

The popularity of pasta dishes, either as an appetizer, side dish, an ingredient in soups, as a main course or even as a dessert, cannot be over emphasized.

The ease of putting a pasta-based meal and pulling it off probably has a lot to do with its popularity. One thing that is not in question though, is the love of pasta even among different social groups of persons and across all ages.

Pasta is an appealing and tasty delicacy and is extremely enjoyable to eat, put together and combine with almost all types of food classes enjoyed by mankind.